CURIOUS CATS

CURIOUS CATS

MITSUAKI IWAGO

CHRONICLE BOOKS

SAN FRANCISCO

First published in the United States in 2010 by Chronicle Books LLC.

Photographs © 2005, 2008 by Mitsuaki Iwago.
English translation © 2010 by Mitsuaki Iwago.
Photographs originally published by Shogakukan Inc., Tokyo, Japan,
in 2005 as *Chotto Neko Boke* and in 2008 as *Sotto Neko Boke*.
English translation rights arranged with Shogakukan Inc. through
Tuttle-Mori Agency, Inc.

Library of Congress Cataloging-in-Publication data available.
ISBN 978-0-8118-7004-7

Manufactured in China.

Designed by Sarah O'Rourke and Wilfred Castillo.

10 9 8 7 6 5 4 3 2 1

Chronicle Books LLC
680 Second Street
San Francisco, California 94107
www.chroniclebooks.com

INTRODUCTION

In my career as a professional photographer, I have traveled the world taking pictures of all sorts of animals—from elephants in the African plains to penguins and snow monkeys—and observed them in their natural habitats. But even after seeing all of these exotic species, none has captured my attention and my heart as much as cats.

After observing the endless energy and exuberance of cats while photographing them for this collection, I came to realize that there is truly no limit to a cat's playing. Whether they're leaping from a tree or exploring a new corner of the house, cats are always up to something. Even when they are just napping in a square of sunlight on the floor they seem to have a serene quality that makes me love to watch them. In these carefully chosen photographs, I have captured cats in their moments of liveliness and repose, excitement and solitude, to truly paint a picture of my love for their species.

I have handpicked what I believe to be the finest—and cutest!—kitty shots to share, from my collection of over thirty years' worth of photographs. I hope that cat lovers everywhere will be delighted with these playful and elegant cats. Because as I always say, when cats are happy, people are happy, and the world is happy.

—Mitsuaki Iwago

What makes a cat a cat is the ability to find anything.

SPRINGTIME is the perfect time for exploring . . .

Do not disturb.

GREETINGS AND SALUTATIONS are very important.

Never let your guard down.

PEEKABOO!

Rubbing heads together is a sign of friendship and a way of communication.

Please teach me the way
to move gracefully.

...ACTING SEXY...

When people are busy, cats are busy, too.

Cats act surprising every day.

There is no limit to a cat's play.

It's quite hot today...

THE WORLD is our playground. Even if it's just a pile of wood.

PATIENCE.

Here comes the rainy season.

I guess this too can be called a type of love.

SNOW makes a good snack.

A cat moves beautifully through a snow field, in the morning sunlight.

A cat's passion is concentration.

Perhaps cats are yearning for a quieter world, too.